DEMENTIA CAREGIVER GUIDE

Your Essential Resource for Dementia Caregiving Success, With Practical Insights for Managing Dementia Day-to-Day

Lori J. Carter

Copyright © 2024 by Lori J. Carter

TABLE OF CONTENTS

INTRODUCTION

When my mother was diagnosed with dementia, our lives changed forever. I was thrust into the role of caregiver, unprepared for the emotional and physical challenges that lay ahead. It was a journey filled with confusion, frustration, and many sleepless nights. But it was also a journey of love, patience, and small victories.

I remember the day I first noticed something was wrong. Mom was always sharp as a tack, but she started forgetting simple things like where she put her keys or the name of a close friend. At first, we laughed it off, thinking it was just part of aging. But as her forgetfulness grew worse, our laughter turned to worry. When the diagnosis came, it hit us hard. We felt lost and overwhelmed, not knowing what to expect or how to help her.

In the beginning, I struggled to find the right resources and support. The information out there was either too clinical or too vague, leaving me more confused than before. I wished for a simple, straightforward guide that could walk me through the steps of caring for someone with dementia, offering practical advice and emotional support.

That's why I decided to write this book. I wanted to create the guide I needed when I was starting out, one that could help other caregivers navigate the difficult but rewarding path of caring for a loved one with dementia. This book is not just a collection of tips and strategies; it's a companion for your journey, offering support, understanding, and hope.

Caring for someone with dementia is a journey filled with ups and downs. There will be moments of frustration and sadness, but also times of connection and joy. This guide will walk you through each step, from preparing for the caregiving role to managing daily tasks and handling emotional challenges. You will also learn how to take care of your own health and well-being, which is just as important.

As you go through this guide, remember you are not alone. Many have walked this path before you and have found ways to cope and thrive. My hope is that by sharing what I've learned, you will feel more confident and supported in your caregiving role.

Throughout this book, you will find practical advice on everything from managing daily tasks to coping with the emotional toll of caregiving. I've also included personal stories and insights from my own experience and those of other caregivers, to show you that you are not alone.

Caring for someone with dementia is one of the toughest jobs you'll ever face, but it's also one of the most important. You have the power to make a real difference in your loved one's life, providing them with comfort, dignity, and love.

As you go through this manual, I hope you'll find the information you need to be the best caregiver you can be. More importantly, I hope you'll feel empowered and supported, knowing that you are not alone on this journey.

Now, let's embark on this journey together. Dive into the chapters ahead, and discover the tools, tips, and insights that will help you navigate the challenges and joys of dementia caregiving. Your dedication and compassion can light the way for a better future for your loved one and yourself.

Welcome to the Dementia Caregiver Guide. Let's get started.

CHAPTER 1: UNDERSTANDING DEMENTIA

What is Dementia?

Dementia is not a single disease but a term that describes a group of symptoms affecting memory, thinking, and social abilities severely enough to interfere with daily life. It's caused by damage to brain cells, which affects their ability to communicate with each other. This communication breakdown can lead to a decline in cognitive function, impacting areas such as memory, judgment, language, and problem-solving skills.

When my mother was first diagnosed with dementia, I was overwhelmed by the complexity of the condition. The doctor explained that dementia isn't just about forgetfulness; it's about the loss of cognitive functions that affect daily living. This was a crucial moment for me, as I began to understand that we were dealing with more than just typical aging.

Dementia symptoms can vary greatly, but at least two of the following core mental functions must be significantly impaired for a dementia diagnosis: Memory, Communication and language, Ability to focus and pay attention, Reasoning and judgment, and Visual perception.

Types and Stages of Dementia

Types of Dementia

Alzheimer's Disease: This is the most common type of dementia, accounting for 60-80% of cases. It's characterized by plaques and tangles in the brain, which lead to the death of brain cells. Symptoms typically begin with mild memory loss and confusion but progress to severe memory impairment, loss of ability to carry out daily tasks, and personality changes.

Vascular Dementia: This type results from conditions that block or reduce blood flow to the brain, depriving brain cells of vital oxygen and nutrients. It's often caused by strokes or other blood vessel conditions. Symptoms can vary widely depending on the severity and location of the vascular damage, but common signs include difficulties with problem-solving, slowed thinking, and loss of focus.

Lewy Body Dementia: Characterized by abnormal clumps of protein called Lewy bodies in the brain, this type of dementia shares symptoms with Alzheimer's and Parkinson's diseases. It can cause memory loss, visual hallucinations, and muscle rigidity. Lewy Body Dementia can lead to significant fluctuations in alertness and attention.

Frontotemporal Dementia: This type involves damage to the frontal and temporal lobes of the brain. It often affects people at a younger age and leads to changes in personality, behavior, and language. Memory loss isn't usually the first symptom; instead, individuals may exhibit impulsive behaviors, apathy, or inappropriate actions.

Mixed Dementia: In many older adults, multiple types of dementia-related changes in the brain occur simultaneously, often a combination of Alzheimer's disease and vascular dementia. Symptoms may be a blend of both conditions.

Stages of Dementia

Understanding the stages of dementia can help caregivers anticipate and manage the challenges ahead. While each person's experience with dementia is unique, the progression generally follows a similar pattern.

Mild (Early Stage): Symptoms are often subtle and may be mistaken for normal aging. Individuals might have difficulty recalling recent events, finding the right words, or keeping track of bills. They can still function independently but may need reminders and support.

Moderate (Middle Stage): Symptoms become more noticeable and disabling. Memory loss and confusion increase, making it difficult to perform daily activities without assistance. Individuals may forget personal history, become disoriented, and exhibit changes in personality and behavior. They might also experience difficulty with language and require help with personal care.

Severe (Late Stage): In the late stage of dementia, individuals lose the ability to communicate coherently and require full-time care for daily activities. Memory loss is profound, and physical abilities, including walking and swallowing, may decline. This stage is characterized by a significant need for caregiver support and medical attention.

Symptoms and Diagnosis

Symptoms

The symptoms of dementia can vary depending on the type and stage, but common signs include:

Memory loss: The inability to recall recent lessons, significant dates, or memorable occasions. Repeating questions or relying on memory aids more frequently.

Difficulty with Planning and Problem-Solving: Struggling to develop and follow a plan or work with numbers. difficulty focusing and a noticeable increase in processing time.

Challenges with Completing Familiar Tasks: Problems with completing daily tasks at home, work, or leisure, such as driving to a familiar location or managing a budget.

Time or Place Confusion: Forgetting the seasons, dates, and the passing of time. unable to recall their location or method of travel.

Difficulty Perceiving Color and Contrast: This may lead to issues when driving. It can also cause trouble reading, estimating distance, and understanding visual images and spatial relationships.

New Problems with Words in Speaking or Writing: Struggling with vocabulary, finding the right word, or calling things by the wrong name.

Misplacing Things and Losing the Ability to Retrace Steps: Placing items in unusual places, losing things, and being unable to go back over steps to find them.

Reduced or Poor Judgment: Noticing shifts in one's ability to judge or make decisions. For example, giving large amounts of money to telemarketers or paying less attention to grooming.

Withdrawal from Work or Social Activities: Avoiding social activities, hobbies, or work projects due to the changes they are experiencing.

Changes in Mood and Personality: Becoming confused, suspicious, depressed, fearful, or anxious. Easily upset in unfamiliar places or with unfamiliar people.

Diagnosis

Diagnosing dementia involves a comprehensive assessment. Early diagnosis can help manage symptoms and improve quality of life. The process typically includes:

Medical History: The doctor will ask about symptoms, family medical history, and any medications being taken.

Physical Examination: A thorough physical exam can help rule out other conditions that might be causing symptoms.

Neurological Tests: These tests assess balance, sensory responses, reflexes, and other functions to determine the cause of symptoms.

Cognitive and Neuropsychological Tests: These tests measure memory, problem-solving, language skills, and other cognitive abilities.

Brain Scans: Imaging tests like MRI or CT scans can identify strokes, tumors, or other issues that may cause symptoms.

Laboratory Tests: Blood tests can help rule out other potential causes of symptoms, such as vitamin deficiencies or thyroid problems.

Psychiatric Evaluation: A mental health professional can help determine if depression or another mental health condition is contributing to symptoms.

When my mother began showing signs of dementia, the diagnostic process was thorough. Her doctor conducted multiple tests and evaluations to rule out other conditions. It was a lengthy and sometimes stressful process, but getting a clear diagnosis was crucial for developing an effective care plan.

The Impact on Individuals and Families

Dementia affects not only the individual diagnosed but also their families and caregivers. The emotional, physical, and financial toll can be significant, and understanding these impacts can help in preparing and managing the caregiving journey.

Emotional Impact

For the individual with dementia, the emotional impact can include fear, confusion, frustration, and depression. They may be aware of their declining abilities, leading to anxiety and a sense of loss. It's essential for caregivers to provide emotional support, reassurance, and a sense of security.

Families often experience a range of emotions, including sadness, grief, and even anger. Watching a loved one change and lose their abilities is heartbreaking. Caregivers may also feel overwhelmed by the responsibility and the constant demands on their time and energy.

I vividly remember the emotional rollercoaster I went through with my mother. There were days when she seemed almost like her old self, and then there were days when she didn't recognize me. The emotional swings were challenging, but I found that talking to others in similar situations helped me cope.

Physical Impact

The physical demands of caregiving can be exhausting. Assisting with daily activities, managing medications, and handling behavioral issues can take a toll on caregivers' health. Many caregivers experience fatigue, sleep problems, and stress-related illnesses.

For the person with dementia, physical health often declines as the disease progresses. They may have difficulty with coordination, mobility, and eventually, even basic functions like eating and swallowing.

Financial Impact

Dementia care can be expensive. Costs include medical treatments, medications, home modifications, and possibly long-term care facilities. Many families face financial strain and may need to explore options like insurance, government assistance, or community resources.

When my mother needed more specialized care, we had to consider long-term care facilities, which were costly. Navigating the financial aspects of dementia care was daunting, but we found that seeking advice from financial advisors and support organizations was beneficial.

Social Impact

Dementia can lead to social isolation for both the individual and their caregivers. The person with dementia may withdraw from social activities due to embarrassment or difficulty communicating. Caregivers might also isolate themselves because of the demands of caregiving and the lack of time for social interactions.

Maintaining social connections is crucial for mental health. I made it a priority to involve friends and family in my mother's care, ensuring she still had social interactions and support. It wasn't always easy, but it made a significant difference in her well-being and mine.

Coping and Support

Finding ways to cope with the impacts of dementia is essential for both individuals and caregivers. Counseling, support groups, and educational materials can all be very helpful. Sharing experiences with others who understand what you're going through can be incredibly comforting and informative.

As a caregiver, I joined a local support group for families dealing with dementia. It was a lifeline during tough times, offering a space to share frustrations, seek advice, and learn from others. The connections I made there were invaluable, reminding me that I wasn't alone.

Dementia is a complex and challenging condition that affects every aspect of life for those diagnosed and their families. Understanding what dementia is, the types and stages, symptoms, diagnosis, and its impact can help you prepare for the journey ahead. This knowledge is the first step in becoming an effective and compassionate caregiver.

In the following chapters, we will delve deeper into the practical aspects of caregiving, offering strategies, tips, and resources to help you navigate this journey. Remember, you are not alone. There is a community of caregivers, professionals, and resources ready to support you. Together, we can provide the best care possible for our loved ones with dementia.

Let's move forward with hope, resilience, and the knowledge that we can make a difference. Dive into the next chapter to begin equipping yourself with the tools and insights needed for this important journey.

CHAPTER 2: PREPARING FOR THE CAREGIVING ROLE

Preparing to care for a loved one with dementia is a multifaceted task that requires emotional readiness, practical planning, and a supportive environment. This chapter will guide you through the key areas you need to address to be well-prepared for the caregiving role: emotional readiness, building a support network, legal and financial planning, and home safety and modifications. Drawing from my own experiences, I will provide practical advice and insights to help you navigate this journey with confidence and compassion.

Emotional Readiness

Taking on the role of a caregiver for a loved one with dementia is a significant emotional undertaking. It demands a great deal of tolerance, compassion, and fortitude. Before diving into the practical aspects of caregiving, it's essential to assess and cultivate your emotional readiness.

Understanding Your Emotions

When my mother was diagnosed with dementia, I experienced a whirlwind of emotions: fear, sadness, anger, and even guilt. It's crucial to recognize that these feelings are normal and valid. Caregiving is an emotional journey, and acknowledging your feelings is the first step in managing them.

Fear and Anxiety: The uncertainty of what lies ahead can be daunting. Fear of the unknown, fear of not being able to provide adequate care, and anxiety about the future are common. Understanding that these feelings are part of the process can help you approach caregiving with a clearer mind.

Sadness and Grief: Watching a loved one change and decline is heart-wrenching. It's important to allow yourself to grieve these losses, both big and small. Grieving is not a one-time event but a recurring process as you face new challenges.

Anger and Frustration: The demands of caregiving can lead to feelings of frustration and anger. These emotions might be directed at the situation, the disease, or even at the person you are caring for. Finding healthy ways to express and manage these feelings is crucial.

Guilt and Self-Doubt: Many caregivers struggle with guilt, feeling they are not doing enough or making mistakes. It's important to remind yourself that you are doing your best in a challenging situation. Perfection is not the goal; providing compassionate care is.

Developing Emotional Resilience

Building emotional resilience will help you manage the ups and downs of caregiving. I was able to use the following tactics:

Self-Care: Taking care of your own physical and mental health is paramount. This means ensuring you get enough sleep, eat well, and find time for activities you enjoy. Regular exercise and mindfulness practices, such as meditation or yoga, can also be beneficial.

Realistic Expectations: Recognize that you are not able to accomplish everything flawlessly. Establish reasonable objectives for both you and your partner. Do not focus on failures and instead acknowledge small successes.

Seeking Professional Help: Don't hesitate to seek help from a therapist or counselor. Professional support can provide a safe space to express your feelings and develop coping strategies.

Finding Joy: Look for moments of joy and connection with your loved one. These moments can provide emotional sustenance and remind you why you are on this journey.

Preparing for Emotional Challenges

Caregiving will bring emotional challenges, and being prepared can make a difference. Here are some scenarios that you may encounter:

Role Reversal: It can be difficult to care for a parent or older relative, as it reverses the traditional roles. This shift can bring feelings of discomfort and sadness. Acknowledge these feelings and seek support to navigate this transition.

Dealing with Difficult Behaviors: Dementia can cause challenging behaviors, such as aggression, confusion, and wandering. Learning strategies to manage these behaviors will help reduce stress. The most important things are empathy, patience, and good conversation.

Managing Family Dynamics: Caregiving can strain family relationships. Open communication and setting boundaries are essential. Involve family members in care decisions and delegate tasks to share the load.

When my mother's condition started to decline, I often felt overwhelmed. I found that talking to friends and joining a support group made a significant difference. Sharing experiences and hearing from others who were on a similar path provided comfort and practical advice. I also learned to set aside time for myself, even if it was just a short walk or reading a book. These small acts of self-care recharged my emotional batteries and made me a more effective caregiver.

Building a Support Network

No one should have to navigate caregiving alone. Building a robust support network is crucial for both your well-being and the quality of care you provide. A support network can include family, friends, healthcare professionals, and community resources.

Involving Family and Friends

Caring for a loved one with dementia is often a family affair. Involving family and friends can provide practical help and emotional support.

Open Communication: Keep family and friends informed about your loved one's condition and needs. Regular updates can help them understand the situation and how they can assist.

Delegating Tasks: Don't be afraid to ask for help. Assign specific tasks to family members or friends, such as running errands, providing respite care, or helping with household chores. Clear communication about what you need can make it easier for others to contribute.

Emotional Support: Sometimes, you just need someone to listen. Seek out emotional support from family members and trusted friends. Sharing your experiences and feelings can alleviate stress.

Professional Support

Healthcare professionals play a vital role in the caregiving journey. Building a relationship with your loved one's medical team can provide essential guidance and support.

Primary Care Physician: Maintain regular communication with your loved one's primary care physician. They can help monitor the progression of dementia and manage other health conditions.

Specialists: Depending on the type and stage of dementia, consulting specialists such as neurologists, psychiatrists, or geriatricians can be beneficial. They can provide specific care and treatment.

Home Health Care Services: Hiring home health aides or nurses can provide additional support, especially for medical tasks and personal care. These professionals can also offer respite for primary caregivers.

Community Resources

Many communities offer resources and services for caregivers and individuals with dementia. These can include:

Support Groups: Joining a support group can provide a sense of community and a space to share experiences and advice. Look for local or online groups that focus on dementia caregiving.

Adult Day Care Centers: These centers provide supervised care and activities for individuals with dementia, offering caregivers a break during the day.

Respite Care Services: Temporary respite care services can give caregivers a much-needed break. This can be provided in-home, at a care facility, or through adult day programs.

Nonprofit Organizations: Organizations such as the Alzheimer's Association offer a wealth of resources, including educational materials, support groups, and helplines.

In the early stages of my mother's dementia, I tried to handle everything on my own. It didn't take long to realize that I needed help. Reaching out to family and friends, even for small tasks, made a big difference. I also connected with a local support group, where I met other caregivers who shared their experiences and advice. This network became a lifeline, providing practical help and emotional support when I needed it most.

Legal and Financial Planning

Legal and financial planning is a critical aspect of preparing for the caregiving role. Addressing these issues early can prevent future complications and ensure that your loved one's wishes are honored.

Legal Planning

Legal planning involves making decisions about healthcare, finances, and personal wishes. It's important to involve your loved one in these discussions while they are still able to communicate their preferences.

Durable Power of Attorney (POA): A POA allows your loved one to appoint someone to make financial and legal decisions on their behalf if they become incapacitated. This person, known as the agent, can manage bank accounts, pay bills, and handle other financial matters.

Healthcare Power of Attorney: This legal document designates someone to make healthcare decisions if your loved one is unable to do so. It's crucial to choose a person who understands your loved one's wishes and values.

Living Will: A living will outlines your loved one's preferences for end-of-life care, including decisions about life-sustaining treatments. This document can guide healthcare providers and family members during difficult decisions.

Last Will and Testament: This document specifies how your loved one's assets and property will be distributed after their death. It can also designate guardians for minor children or dependents.

Advance Directives: Advance directives include both the healthcare power of attorney and living will. They provide instructions for medical care and designate a healthcare agent.

Financial Planning

Dementia care can be expensive, and financial planning is essential to manage these costs. Consider the following steps:

Budgeting: Create a budget that includes all potential expenses related to dementia care, such as medical treatments, home modifications, and caregiving services. Review and adjust the budget regularly as needs change.

Insurance: Review existing insurance policies, including health, long-term care, and life insurance.Recognize the coverage and, if needed, take into account acquiring supplemental insurance..

Government Assistance: Explore eligibility for government programs such as Medicaid, Medicare, and Social Security Disability Insurance (SSDI). These programs can provide financial assistance for medical care and living expenses.

Estate Planning: Consult with an estate planning attorney to create a comprehensive plan that includes wills, trusts, and other legal tools to manage assets and protect your loved one's financial interests.

Financial Advisors: Working with a financial advisor who specializes in elder care can help you navigate the complexities of financial planning. They can provide guidance on investments, retirement planning, and managing expenses.

Navigating the legal and financial aspects of dementia care was daunting at first, but I quickly realized its importance. I consulted with an attorney to create power of attorney documents and a living will for my mother. We also reviewed her financial situation and made adjustments to ensure she had access to the resources she needed for care. Having these plans in place gave me peace of mind and ensured that my mother's wishes were honored.

Home Safety and Modifications

Creating a safe and supportive environment at home is essential for individuals with dementia. Simple modifications can help prevent accidents and promote independence while providing peace of mind for caregivers.

Assessing Home Safety

Begin by evaluating your loved one's home for potential hazards. Look for:

Fall Risks: Remove tripping hazards such as rugs, cords, and clutter. Install grab bars and handrails in high-risk areas such as bathrooms and staircases.

Wandering Risks: Secure doors and windows to prevent wandering. Consider installing door alarms or GPS tracking devices for added security.

Fire and Electrical Safety: Ensure smoke detectors are working properly and install carbon monoxide detectors if necessary. Check electrical outlets and appliances for signs of damage or malfunction.

Medication Safety: Keep medications in a secure location out of reach of children and individuals with dementia. Consider using pill organizers or automatic medication dispensers to manage doses.

Home Modifications

Making simple modifications to the home can enhance safety and accessibility for individuals with dementia. Consider:

Lighting: Ensure adequate lighting throughout the home to reduce confusion and improve visibility. Install motion-activated lights in hallways and bathrooms for added safety at night.

Bathroom Safety: Install grab bars in the shower and near the toilet to assist with balance and mobility.For more stability, think about using a bench or shower chair.

Kitchen Safety: Remove clutter from countertops and ensure that commonly used items are easily accessible. Consider installing safety knobs on stove burners and childproof locks on cabinets containing hazardous items.

Bedroom Safety: Place a nightlight near the bed to prevent falls during nighttime trips to the bathroom. Ensure that the bed is at a comfortable height for easy entry and exit.

Accessibility: Make sure that the home is easily navigable for individuals with mobility issues. Remove obstacles and arrange furniture to create clear pathways.

Assistive Devices and Technology

Advances in technology have made it easier to monitor and support individuals with dementia at home. Consider:

Medical Alert Systems: These systems allow individuals to call for help in the event of an emergency. Some systems include fall detection and GPS tracking features for added security.

Smart Home Devices: Smart home devices such as voice-activated assistants and remote-controlled thermostats can enhance independence and safety for individuals with dementia.

GPS Tracking Devices: GPS tracking devices can be worn or attached to clothing or accessories to monitor the whereabouts of individuals with dementia who are at risk of wandering.

Home Monitoring Systems: Video monitoring systems can provide peace of mind for caregivers by allowing them to check on their loved one remotely. Some systems include motion sensors and alerts for unusual activity.

Making modifications to my mother's home was an essential step in ensuring her safety and well-being. We installed grab bars in the bathroom and made sure there was adequate lighting throughout the house. Simple changes, like removing clutter and rearranging furniture, made it easier for her to navigate the space independently. These modifications gave both of us peace of mind and allowed her to remain at home for as long as possible.

Preparing for the caregiving role involves emotional readiness, building a support network, legal and financial planning, and home safety and modifications. By addressing these areas proactively, you can provide the best possible care for your loved one with dementia while maintaining your own well-being. In the following chapters, we will explore practical strategies for managing daily caregiving tasks, communicating effectively, and finding joy in the caregiving journey. On this journey, never forget that you are not alone. Reach out for support when you need it, and take care of yourself as you care for others.

CHAPTER 3: DAILY CAREGIVING TASKS

Caring for a loved one with dementia involves a variety of daily tasks that require patience, compassion, and a strategic approach. This chapter will guide you through essential aspects of daily caregiving: personal care (bathing, dressing, and hygiene), managing medications, nutrition and meal planning, and creating a routine. By mastering these tasks, you can provide better care for your loved one while also making your caregiving role more manageable and fulfilling.

Personal Care: Bathing, Dressing, and Hygiene

Personal care is a fundamental part of caregiving that significantly impacts your loved one's comfort and dignity. Ensuring they are clean, well-dressed, and maintaining good hygiene helps prevent infections and boosts their self-esteem.

Bathing

Bathing can be a challenging task for caregivers and can be a source of anxiety for individuals with dementia. It's important to approach this task with sensitivity and preparation.

Creating a Safe Environment: Ensure the bathroom is safe by installing grab bars, using non-slip mats, and having all necessary bathing supplies within reach. The water temperature should be warm, not hot, to avoid burns.

Routine and Consistency: Establish a regular bathing schedule that suits your loved one's preferences. Consistency can reduce anxiety and resistance. Bathing in the morning or evening, depending on their routine, can make the process smoother.

Communicating Clearly: Explain each step of the process in simple terms. Use gentle reassurances to keep them calm. For example, "Now we're going to wash your hands. Doesn't the warm water feel nice?"

Promoting Independence: Encourage your loved one to do as much as they can on their own. This promotes independence and maintains their abilities. For instance, you can hand them a washcloth and ask them to wash their face while you assist with the harder-to-reach areas.

Maintaining Dignity: Always protect their privacy and dignity by covering them with a towel or bathrobe when they are undressing or getting out of the bath. Using a handheld shower head can make rinsing easier and more comfortable.

Dressing

Dressing can also be a challenging task, but it provides an excellent opportunity to encourage independence and self-expression.

Choosing Comfortable Clothing: Select clothes that are comfortable, easy to put on, and suitable for the weather. Opt for items with simple fastenings like Velcro or zippers instead of buttons.

Simplifying Choices: Limit the number of clothing choices to avoid overwhelming them. For example, you can lay out two outfits and let them choose which one they want to wear.

Step-by-Step Guidance: Break down the dressing process into simple steps. Use prompts and cues, such as, "Now let's put on your shirt," to guide them through each step.

Adaptive Clothing: Consider adaptive clothing designed for people with mobility issues or cognitive impairments. These garments are often easier to put on and take off, reducing frustration.

Encouragement and Patience: Provide encouragement and praise for their efforts, regardless of how much help they need. Patience is key; rushing can lead to frustration for both of you.

Hygiene

Keeping oneself clean is essential for overall health and wellbeing. It includes tasks like brushing teeth, grooming, and using the toilet.

Oral Care: Ensure that your loved one brushes their teeth at least twice a day. Use a soft-bristled toothbrush and fluoride toothpaste. If they struggle with brushing, try an electric toothbrush or provide hand-over-hand assistance.

Hair Care: Regularly wash and brush their hair to prevent tangles and promote scalp health. Consider a hairstyle that is easy to manage.

Nail Care: Keep nails trimmed to prevent scratching and reduce the risk of infections. If they are unable to tolerate nail trimming, seek help from a professional.

Toileting: Establish a regular toileting schedule to prevent accidents. Make sure the bathroom is easy to access, and consider using adaptive equipment like raised toilet seats or commodes. Always respect their privacy and provide assistance as needed.

When my mother's dementia progressed, personal care became more challenging. Bathing was particularly difficult due to her fear of water. I learned that playing soothing music and using a handheld shower head made the experience less stressful for her. Dressing also required patience;

choosing simple outfits and breaking down the steps helped maintain her dignity and independence. Remember, these tasks are about more than just physical care—they are about showing respect and love.

Managing Medications

Managing medications is a critical aspect of caregiving that ensures your loved one receives the correct dosages at the right times. Proper medication management can prevent health complications and improve their quality of life.

Organizing Medications

Medication List: Keep an up-to-date list of all medications, including dosages, frequency, and prescribing doctors. This list should be easily accessible in case of emergencies.

Pill Organizers: Arrange prescription drugs according to day and time with pill organizers. This helps prevent missed doses and reduces the risk of overdose.

Medication Schedule: Create a medication schedule and display it in a visible location. Consistency is key, so try to administer medications at the same times each day.

Administering Medications

Simple Instructions: Provide clear, simple instructions when giving medications. For example, "Here is your pill for blood pressure. Please take it with a glass of water."

Monitoring Compliance: Observe your loved one taking their medication to ensure compliance. Some individuals with dementia may forget or refuse to take their medications.

Managing Side Effects: Be aware of potential side effects and interactions. Monitor your loved one for any changes in behavior or health that could be related to their medications.

Working with Healthcare Professionals

Regular Reviews: Schedule regular reviews with healthcare professionals to assess the effectiveness of medications and make any necessary adjustments. Talk about any worries or adverse effects right away.

Pharmacy Support: Utilize the services of your local pharmacy. Pharmacists can provide valuable information on medication management, potential interactions, and reminders for refills.

Handling Medication Refusal

Understanding Reasons: If your loved one refuses to take their medication, try to understand the reasons. It could be due to a bad taste, difficulty swallowing, or confusion about the medication's purpose.

Alternative Forms: Discuss with the healthcare provider about alternative forms of the medication, such as liquid, patch, or dissolvable tablets.

Positive Reinforcement: Use positive reinforcement and gentle encouragement to persuade them. Avoid confrontation, as it can increase resistance.

Managing my mother's medications required meticulous organization and consistency. We used a weekly pill organizer and a medication chart to keep track of her dosages. On occasions when she refused to take her pills, I discovered that offering them with a favorite drink or during a calm moment helped. Building a good relationship with her pharmacist provided additional support and ensured we stayed on top of her medication regimen.

Nutrition and Meal Planning

Proper nutrition is essential for maintaining health and well-being, especially for individuals with dementia. Planning and preparing balanced meals can be challenging, but with the right strategies, you can ensure your loved one gets the nutrients they need.

Understanding Nutritional Needs

Balanced Diet: Focus on providing a balanced diet that includes a variety of fruits, vegetables, whole grains, lean proteins, and healthy fats. This supports overall health and can improve cognitive function.

Hydration: Ensure your loved one stays hydrated by encouraging regular fluid intake. Dehydration can exacerbate dementia symptoms and lead to other health issues.

Special Dietary Needs: Be aware of any special dietary needs or restrictions, such as diabetes, heart conditions, or food allergies. Make meal plans that take these needs into account.

Meal Planning

Simple and Nutritious Meals: Plan simple, nutritious meals that are easy to prepare and eat. Avoid complex recipes that may be difficult for your loved one to understand or consume.

Consistency and Routine: Establish regular meal times to create a predictable routine. This can reduce confusion and help stimulate appetite.

Small, Frequent Meals: If large meals are overwhelming, consider offering small, frequent meals and snacks throughout the day.

Involving Your Loved One: When possible, involve your loved one in meal planning and preparation. This can increase their interest in food and provide a sense of accomplishment.

Creating a Positive Mealtime Environment

Minimize Distractions: Create a calm, distraction-free environment during meals. Turn off the television, remove clutter from the table, and reduce noise levels.

Simple Table Settings: Use simple, uncluttered table settings. Choose plates and utensils that are easy to handle. High-contrast colors between the plate and the food can help with visual perception.

Encouraging Independence: Encourage your loved one to feed themselves as much as possible. Offer assistance when needed but try to promote independence.

Addressing Eating Challenges

Loss of Appetite: Dementia can affect appetite. Encourage small, nutrient-dense snacks and monitor weight to ensure they are getting enough calories.

Difficulty Swallowing: If your loved one has difficulty swallowing (dysphagia), consult a healthcare provider for a swallowing assessment. They may recommend texture-modified diets or thickened liquids.

Behavioral Difficulties: Be patient and understanding when handling any behavioral difficulties, such as pacing during meals or refusing to eat. Offer finger foods or smaller portions to make eating less daunting.

Ensuring my mother received proper nutrition was a constant effort. We developed a meal routine that included her favorite foods, which helped maintain her interest in eating. Introducing finger foods and small, frequent meals made it easier for her to eat independently. Patience and creativity were key in overcoming challenges, like loss of appetite and difficulty swallowing.

Creating a Routine

Creating a routine is beneficial for both the caregiver and the individual with dementia. A predictable routine can reduce anxiety, improve cooperation, and create a sense of stability.

Establishing a Daily Routine

Consistent Schedule: Establish a consistent daily schedule that includes regular times for waking up, meals, activities, and bedtime. Consistency helps reduce confusion and anxiety.

Structured Activities: Plan structured activities throughout the day, such as exercise, hobbies, and social interactions. Engaging in meaningful activities can enhance mood and cognitive function.

Balanced Rest: Ensure that the routine includes time for rest and relaxation. Avoid over-scheduling, which can lead to fatigue and frustration.

Incorporating Personal Preferences

Personal Interests: Incorporate your loved one's personal interests and preferences into the daily routine. Whether it's listening to music, gardening, or painting, engaging in enjoyable activities can improve their quality of life.

Flexibility: It is essential to be flexible in addition to being consistent. Be prepared to adjust the routine based on your loved one's needs and energy levels.

Using Visual Cues

Visual Schedules: Use visual schedules or calendars to outline the daily routine. Simple pictures and words can serve as helpful reminders for tasks and activities.

Environmental Cues: Arrange the home environment to support the routine. For example, placing grooming supplies in a visible, accessible spot can cue your loved one to brush their teeth.

Dealing with Changes and Transitions

Advance Notice: Give advance notice of any changes or transitions in the routine. This can help reduce anxiety and make the transition smoother.

Gradual Adjustments: Introduce changes gradually. Sudden changes can be overwhelming and may lead to increased confusion or resistance.

Creating a consistent routine was instrumental in managing my mother's daily care. We developed a schedule that included her favorite activities, regular meal times, and rest periods. Visual cues, like a daily calendar with pictures, helped her understand and anticipate what was coming next. This routine provided structure and stability, making both our lives more predictable and less stressful.

Mastering daily caregiving tasks—personal care, managing medications, nutrition and meal planning, and creating a routine—is essential for providing effective and compassionate care for your loved one with dementia. By approaching these tasks with patience, organization, and empathy, you can improve their quality of life and make your caregiving role more manageable. In the next chapter, we will explore strategies for effective communication and managing challenging behaviors. Remember, each day is an opportunity to show love and support in meaningful ways.

CHAPTER 4: COMMUNICATION STRATEGIES

Effective communication is crucial in dementia care, fostering understanding, reducing frustration, and enhancing the quality of life for both the caregiver and the person with dementia. This chapter will cover effective communication techniques, handling difficult conversations, understanding non-verbal cues, and enhancing social interaction. Through my personal experiences and practical tips, you will learn how to communicate more effectively and compassionately with your loved one.

Effective Communication Techniques

Communicating with someone who has dementia requires patience, empathy, and clear strategies. Here are some effective communication techniques:

Simplify Language

Use Simple Words and Sentences: Avoid complex sentences and jargon. Instead, use straightforward language. For example, instead of saying, "Let's proceed with our morning routine," say, "It's time to get dressed."

Speak Slowly and Clearly: Ensure that you speak at a moderate pace and enunciate your words clearly. This helps your loved one process what you are saying.

Be Patient and Supportive

Allow Time for Response: Give your loved one enough time to respond. Don't rush them or finish their sentences. Patience is key.

Encourage Conversation: Show interest in their responses, even if they are off-topic. Encourage them to express themselves without correcting them frequently.

Use Positive and Reassuring Language

Remain Calm: To foster a supportive atmosphere, speak in a soothing, upbeat manner. Say something like, "Let us try this instead," rather than, "Do not do that."

Avoid Negative Phrases: Phrases like "You're wrong" or "No, that's not right" can be discouraging. Focus on what they can do and provide gentle guidance.

Clarify and Repeat

Repeat Key Points: Sometimes, repeating important information can help with comprehension. Use the same words and phrases to reinforce understanding.

Rephrase if Necessary: If your loved one doesn't understand something, try rephrasing it. Simplify the sentence or use different words.

Minimize Distractions

Create a Quiet Environment: Reduce background noise and distractions. Turn off the TV, radio, or any other noise sources when having a conversation.

Maintain Eye Contact: Establishing eye contact can help your loved one focus on you and understand that you are communicating with them.

Use Visual Aids

Show, Don't Just Tell: Whenever possible, use visual aids to supplement your words. For instance, if you are asking if they want to eat, show them the food options.

Gestures and Expressions: Use hand gestures and facial expressions to convey your message. These non-verbal cues can enhance understanding.

When my mother's dementia advanced, communicating with her became increasingly challenging. I found that simplifying my language and using clear, positive phrases made a significant difference. For example, when asking her to do something, I would break it down into small, manageable steps. If she didn't understand, I patiently rephrased my request. Creating a quiet, distraction-free environment also helped her focus better on our conversations.

Handling Difficult Conversations

Difficult conversations are inevitable in dementia care. Whether discussing sensitive topics or managing behavioral issues, these conversations require a delicate approach.

Approach with Empathy

Understand Their Perspective: Try to see things from your loved one's point of view. Recognize their feelings and validate their emotions.

Stay Calm and Composed: Your demeanor can influence the outcome of the conversation. Stay calm, composed, and avoid showing frustration.

Choose the Right Time and Place

Timing is Key: Choose a time when your loved one is most alert and calm. Avoid having difficult conversations when they are tired, agitated, or hungry.

Private and Comfortable Setting: Ensure the setting is private and comfortable. A familiar environment can make difficult conversations less intimidating.

Be Clear and Direct

Use Clear, Direct Language: Be honest and direct, but also gentle. Avoid sugar-coating or giving false reassurances. For example, if discussing health concerns, say, "We need to talk about your health and how we can make you feel better."

Break Down Information: Provide information in small, digestible chunks. This makes it easier for them to understand and process what you are saying.

Prepare for Emotional Reactions

Expect Emotions: Be prepared for a range of emotional reactions, including anger, sadness, or denial. Acknowledge their feelings and provide comfort.

Stay Patient: If your loved one becomes upset, stay patient and offer reassurance. Sometimes, taking a break and revisiting the conversation later can help.

Use a Supportive Tone

Encouragement: Throughout the talk, adopt a kind and encouraging tone. Reassure them that you are there to help and support them.

Offer Solutions: Focus on finding solutions together. For example, if discussing a move to a care facility, highlight the benefits and how it can improve their quality of life.

One of the hardest conversations I had with my mother was about her no longer driving. She was fiercely independent and loved her car. I chose a calm morning and started by acknowledging how important driving was to her. I explained the safety concerns and reassured her that we would find other ways for her to get around. Although it was a difficult conversation, approaching it with empathy, patience, and clear, direct language helped us navigate the emotional challenge.

Understanding Non-Verbal Cues

Non-verbal communication plays a significant role in interacting with individuals with dementia. Understanding and interpreting these cues can enhance communication and foster a deeper connection.

Reading Facial Expressions

Facial Cues: Pay attention to facial expressions, as they can convey emotions that words may not. A smile, frown, or look of confusion can provide valuable insights into how your loved one is feeling.

Mirroring Emotions: Mirror their emotions to show understanding and empathy. If they look sad, acknowledge their sadness and offer comfort.

Observing Body Language

Posture and Movement: Notice their posture and movements. Slumped shoulders or restless movements can indicate discomfort, anxiety, or pain.

Touch: Gentle touch can convey warmth and reassurance. Holding hands, a gentle pat on the back, or a hug can provide comfort and connection.

Interpreting Gestures

Hand Gestures: Pay attention to hand gestures, which can complement verbal communication.

Pointing, waving, or other gestures can help convey their needs or desires.

Nervous Habits: Be aware of nervous habits or repetitive behaviors, such as fidgeting or pacing. These can indicate stress or discomfort.

Listening to Tone of Voice

Vocal Cues: Tone, pitch, and volume of voice can convey emotions and intentions. A raised voice might indicate frustration, while a soft tone can show affection or concern.

Consistency: Ensure your tone of voice matches your words. Mixed signals can confuse your loved one.

Using Non-Verbal Communication

Demonstrate Actions: Sometimes, demonstrating an action can be more effective than explaining it. For example, showing how to brush teeth rather than just describing it.

Visual Aids: Use pictures, gestures, and objects to support your communication. Visual aids can help clarify your message and make it more understandable.

I learned the importance of non-verbal cues through my interactions with my mother. Often, her facial expressions and body language told me more than her words. For instance, if she appeared agitated and was pacing, I knew she was anxious. A gentle touch and a calming voice often helped soothe her. By paying close attention to her non-verbal signals, I could better understand her needs and respond appropriately.

Enhancing Social Interaction

Maintaining social interaction is vital for individuals with dementia. It helps reduce feelings of isolation, stimulates cognitive function, and improves emotional well-being.

Encouraging Participation in Activities

Meaningful Activities: Encourage participation in activities that they enjoy and find meaningful. This could be anything from gardening to playing music or painting.

Group Activities: Engage them in group activities that promote social interaction. Activities like bingo, crafts, or group exercises can be enjoyable and provide social stimulation.

Creating Opportunities for Interaction

Regular Visits: Arrange regular visits from family and friends. Familiar faces and voices can provide comfort and joy.

Community Involvement: Get them involved in neighborhood activities or senior citizen programs meant for dementia sufferers. Opportunities to socialize and make new friends are presented by this.

Using Technology

Video Calls: Use technology like video calls to stay connected with distant family members and friends. Seeing loved ones can brighten their day and reduce feelings of isolation.

Social Media: If they are comfortable with it, help them use social media to connect with friends and family. Sharing photos and messages can enhance their sense of community.

Adapting Social Interactions

Short and Simple Interactions: Keep social interactions short and simple. Long conversations can be overwhelming and exhausting for individuals with dementia.

Familiar Topics: Discuss familiar topics and past experiences. Reminiscing about happy memories can be comforting and enjoyable.

Encouraging Communication

Ask Open-Ended Questions: Encourage communication by asking open-ended questions that require more than a yes or no answer. For example, "What was your favorite hobby when you were younger?"

Active Listening: Practice active listening by paying full attention to what they are saying. Nod, smile, and respond appropriately to show that you are engaged in the conversation.

Enhancing social interaction was a priority for my mother. We organized weekly visits with family and friends, which she looked forward to. Engaging her in activities like gardening and listening to music brought her joy and provided opportunities for interaction. Technology also played a role; video calls with distant relatives helped her feel connected. By creating a supportive social environment, we improved her emotional well-being and reduced feelings of isolation.

Mastering communication strategies—effective communication techniques, handling difficult conversations, understanding non-verbal cues, and enhancing social interaction—can significantly improve your caregiving experience and the quality of life for your loved one with dementia. Clear, empathetic communication fosters understanding, reduces frustration, and builds stronger connections. In the next chapter, we will explore strategies for managing challenging behaviors. Remember, each interaction is an opportunity to show love, patience, and support.

CHAPTER 5: MANAGING BEHAVIORAL CHALLENGES

Dementia can bring about various behavioral challenges that can be distressing for both the individual and their caregivers. Understanding these behavioral symptoms, developing strategies to manage common issues, coping with sundowning, and knowing when to seek professional help are crucial aspects of providing effective care. In this chapter, we'll explore these topics in detail, incorporating my personal experiences to provide practical insights and advice.

Understanding Behavioral Symptoms

Behavioral symptoms in dementia can vary widely and may change over time. These symptoms can be challenging to manage, but understanding their underlying causes can help you respond more effectively.

Common Behavioral Symptoms

Aggression and Agitation: Individuals with dementia may exhibit aggressive or agitated behaviors, including yelling, hitting, or becoming easily upset.

Wandering: Wandering is a common behavior in dementia, where individuals may roam aimlessly or try to leave their home.

Sundowning: Sundowning refers to increased confusion and agitation during the late afternoon and evening.

Repetition: Repetitive behaviors, such as asking the same question repeatedly, are common in dementia.

Delusions and Hallucinations: Some people may suffer from delusions, which are false beliefs, or hallucinations, which are the seeing or hearing of things that are not there.

Causes of Behavioral Symptoms

Medical Factors: Pain, discomfort, medication side effects, or other medical conditions can contribute to behavioral symptoms.

Environmental Factors: Changes in environment, unfamiliar surroundings, or excessive noise can trigger behavioral issues.

Emotional Factors: Anxiety, fear, frustration, and confusion can lead to behavioral symptoms.

Communication Difficulties: Difficulty expressing needs or understanding others can result in behavioral challenges.

My mother often exhibited agitation and wandering behaviors. Understanding that her agitation was often a result of fear or confusion helped me approach the situation with empathy. When she wandered, I realized it was usually due to her searching for something familiar or trying to fulfill a need, such as looking for a bathroom.

Strategies for Common Issues

Managing behavioral challenges requires patience, creativity, and a range of strategies tailored to the individual's needs. Here, we'll discuss effective strategies for handling aggression, wandering, and other common issues.

Aggression and Agitation

Stay Calm: Respond to aggression with a calm and soothing demeanor. Avoid arguing or raising your voice, as this can escalate the situation.

Identify Triggers: Determine the triggers for aggression. It could be a specific activity, environment, or person. Once recognized, make an effort to avoid or alter these triggers.

Use Distraction: Distract your loved one with a favorite activity or object. Music, a favorite snack, or a walk can help redirect their attention.

Provide Reassurance: Offer verbal and physical reassurance. A gentle touch or calming words can help reduce agitation.

Wandering

Create a Safe Environment: Ensure that the home is safe for wandering. Install locks on doors and windows, and use safety gates if necessary.

Use Visual Cues: Place visual cues around the home to help your loved one find their way. Signs on doors indicating the bathroom or bedroom can be helpful.

Engage in Activities: Keep your loved one engaged in meaningful activities to reduce restlessness and the urge to wander.

Monitor for Patterns: Keep track of when and where wandering occurs. This can help you anticipate and prevent wandering episodes.

Repetition

Stay Patient: Repetitive questions or actions can be frustrating, but it's important to stay patient and respond calmly.

Provide Answers: Answer repetitive questions as if it's the first time. Use consistent and simple responses.

Use Visual Reminders: Visual reminders, such as notes or signs, can help address repetitive questions about daily routines or activities.

Redirect Attention: Gently redirect your loved one's attention to another topic or activity.

Hallucinations and Delusions

Validate Feelings: Validate their feelings without agreeing with the hallucination or delusion. For example, say, "I understand that you're seeing something that's frightening you. I'm here with you."

Ensure Safety: Ensure their safety by removing any objects that could be harmful if they react to a hallucination or delusion.

Distract and Redirect: Use distraction and redirection to shift their focus from the hallucination or delusion to a calming activity.

Consult a Doctor: If hallucinations or delusions are severe or persistent, consult a doctor for evaluation and possible medication adjustments.

Dealing with my mother's wandering was a significant challenge. We installed locks on doors and used visual cues to help her navigate the house safely. Engaging her in activities like folding laundry or sorting buttons kept her occupied and reduced her urge to wander. Her aggression was often a result of frustration, so maintaining a calm demeanor and providing reassurance helped diffuse tense situations.

Coping with Sundowning

Sundowning is a phenomenon where individuals with dementia become more agitated and confused during the late afternoon and evening. Understanding and managing sundowning can improve the quality of life for both the individual and the caregiver.

Understanding Sundowning

Symptoms: Increased confusion, agitation, restlessness, and mood swings are common symptoms of sundowning. These behaviors typically occur in the late afternoon or early evening.

Causes: The exact cause of sundowning is not known, but factors like fatigue, low lighting, and disruptions in the body's internal clock may contribute.

Strategies to Manage Sundowning

Establish a Routine: Maintain a consistent daily routine to provide structure and reduce confusion. Regular meal times, activities, and bedtimes can help.

Increase Daytime Activities: Encourage physical and mental activities during the day to reduce restlessness and promote better sleep at night.

Reduce Stimulation: Minimize noise, bright lights, and other stimuli in the evening. Create a calm and soothing environment.

Provide Comfort: Offer comfort through familiar objects, music, or activities that your loved one finds soothing.

Limit Caffeine and Sugar: Reduce caffeine and sugar intake in the afternoon and evening to prevent increased agitation.

Use Light Therapy: Exposure to natural light during the day and low lighting in the evening can help regulate the body's internal clock.

My mother experienced sundowning, which made the evenings particularly challenging. Establishing a calming evening routine was crucial. We dimmed the lights, played soft music, and engaged in quiet activities like reading or looking at photo albums. Limiting her caffeine intake and ensuring she got plenty of natural light during the day also helped reduce her evening agitation.

When to Seek Professional Help

While many behavioral challenges can be managed at home, there are times when professional help is necessary. Recognizing when to seek outside assistance is essential for the well-being of both the caregiver and the individual with dementia.

Signs You May Need Professional Help

Severe or Persistent Behaviors: If behavioral symptoms are severe, persistent, or pose a danger to your loved one or others, it's time to seek professional help.

Emotional and Physical Strain: If the caregiving role is taking a significant toll on your emotional or physical health, professional assistance can provide much-needed relief.

Lack of Improvement: If you've tried various strategies without improvement, consulting a professional can provide new insights and approaches.

Types of Professional Help

Medical Professionals: Consult a doctor, neurologist, or geriatric psychiatrist for medical evaluations, medication management, and treatment plans.

Therapists: Occupational therapists, physical therapists, and speech therapists can offer strategies to manage behavioral symptoms and improve quality of life.

Counselors: Counselors and social workers can provide emotional support, counseling, and resources for both the caregiver and the individual with dementia.

Support Groups: Joining a support group can provide emotional support, practical advice, and a sense of community with others facing similar challenges.

There were times when my mother's behavioral symptoms were overwhelming. Consulting her doctor helped us adjust her medication, which significantly reduced her agitation. Joining a support group also provided me with emotional support and practical advice from other caregivers. Seeking professional help was a crucial step in managing her symptoms and improving our overall well-being.

Managing behavioral challenges in dementia care requires a combination of understanding, patience, and effective strategies. By understanding the underlying causes of behavioral symptoms, implementing strategies for common issues, coping with sundowning, and knowing when to seek professional help, you can provide compassionate and effective care for your loved one. Remember, each challenge is an opportunity to show love, patience, and support. In the next chapter, we will explore the importance of self-care for caregivers and strategies to maintain your well-being.

CHAPTER 6: EMOTIONAL AND MENTAL HEALTH SUPPORT

Caregiving for a loved one with dementia is a demanding and emotionally taxing role. It's crucial to recognize and address the emotional and mental health challenges that come with caregiving to maintain your well-being. This chapter will explore recognizing caregiver burnout, stress management techniques, finding joy and maintaining well-being, and the importance of support groups and counseling. Drawing from my own experiences, I aim to provide practical advice to help you navigate this journey with resilience and hope.

Recognizing Caregiver Burnout

Caregiver burnout is a state of physical, emotional, and mental exhaustion that can occur when caregivers neglect their own needs while focusing on the needs of their loved ones. Recognizing the signs of burnout early is vital to prevent serious health issues.

Signs of Caregiver Burnout

Physical Symptoms: Constant fatigue, frequent illnesses, headaches, and changes in appetite or sleep patterns.

Emotional Symptoms: Feelings of hopelessness, irritability, sadness, or emotional numbness.

Mental Symptoms: Difficulty concentrating, memory problems, and feeling overwhelmed by caregiving tasks.

Behavioral Symptoms: Absence from social interactions, disregard for one's obligations, and heightened consumption of drugs or alcohol.

Causes of Caregiver Burnout

Role Overload: The constant demands of caregiving without adequate breaks or assistance.

Lack of Support: Feeling isolated or lacking support from family, friends, or professional services.

Emotional Strain: Dealing with the emotional challenges of seeing a loved one's condition deteriorate.

Physical Demands: The physical labor involved in caregiving tasks, such as lifting and assisting with personal care.

In the early stages of my mother's dementia, I threw myself into caregiving, neglecting my own needs. Over time, I began to feel constantly exhausted and emotionally drained. Recognizing these symptoms as burnout was a turning point. I realized that I needed to take care of myself to continue providing the best care for my mother.

Stress Management Techniques

Managing stress effectively is crucial for caregivers to maintain their emotional and mental health. Here are some stress management techniques that can help you stay balanced and resilient.

Practical Stress Management Techniques

Plan Regular Breaks: Allocate time each day for rest and rejuvenation. Quiet time even for a short while can have a significant impact.

Exercise Frequently: Physical activity is a very effective way to relieve stress. Choose a form of exercise that you enjoy doing, such as yoga, dancing, or walking.

Maintain a Healthy Diet: Eating nutritious meals can boost your energy levels and improve your mood. Steer clear of using sugar or caffeine as your go-to sources of energy.

Practice Mindfulness: Mindfulness techniques, such as deep breathing, meditation, or progressive muscle relaxation, can help reduce stress and promote relaxation.

Get Enough Sleep: Try to get 7-8 hours of sleep every night. Create a bedtime routine to help you wind down and improve your sleep quality.

Stay Organized: Keeping a daily schedule and organizing caregiving tasks can help you manage your responsibilities more effectively and reduce feelings of being overwhelmed.

Emotional Stress Management Techniques

Seek Social Support: Stay connected with family and friends. It can be emotionally relieving to share your thoughts and feelings with other people.

Express Your Emotions: Find healthy ways to express your emotions, such as writing in a journal, talking to a friend, or engaging in creative activities like painting or music.

Set Realistic Goals: Set achievable goals and priorities for your caregiving tasks. Put more effort into trying your best rather than aiming for perfection.

Learn to Say No: It's okay to say no to additional responsibilities or requests that add to your stress. Prioritize your own well-being.

Implementing stress management techniques made a significant difference in my ability to cope with caregiving. Regular exercise became my stress outlet, and practicing mindfulness helped me stay present and calm during challenging moments. Seeking social support from friends and family provided emotional relief and a sense of connection.

Finding Joy and Maintaining Well-being

Finding joy and maintaining well-being is essential for caregivers to sustain their role and enhance their quality of life. Here are some strategies to help you find joy amidst the challenges of caregiving.

Cultivating Joy

Focus on Positive Moments: Celebrate small victories and positive moments with your loved one. Cherish the times when they smile, laugh, or show appreciation.

Take Part in Activities You Love: Allocate time for interests and pursuits that offer happiness and satisfaction. Whether it's reading, gardening, or cooking, these activities can provide a much-needed break from caregiving duties.

Spend Time Outdoors: Nature has a calming and rejuvenating effect. Spend time outdoors, whether it's a walk in the park, a hike, or simply sitting in your backyard.

Maintaining Well-being

Prioritize Self-Care: Make self-care a priority. Regularly engage in activities that nurture your body, mind, and spirit.

Set Boundaries: Establish boundaries to protect your personal time and space. Communicate your needs and limits clearly to family members and other caregivers.

Seek Humor: Humor can be a powerful coping mechanism. Find ways to incorporate laughter into your daily routine, whether it's watching a funny movie, reading a humorous book, or sharing jokes with friends.

Finding joy in the little moments helped me stay positive and resilient. My mother loved gardening, and spending time with her in the garden brought both of us immense joy. Taking time for my hobbies, such as reading and painting, also provided a sense of balance and fulfillment.

Support Groups and Counseling

Support groups and counseling can provide invaluable emotional and mental health support for caregivers. Connecting with others who understand your experiences and seeking professional guidance can make a significant difference.

Benefits of Support Groups

Emotional Support: Sharing your experiences with others who understand your challenges can provide emotional relief and a sense of community.

Practical Advice: Support groups often share practical caregiving tips and strategies, which can help you manage your responsibilities more effectively.

Reduced Isolation: Being part of a support group can reduce feelings of isolation and loneliness, providing a network of people who care and understand.

Types of Support Groups

In-Person Groups: Local community centers, hospitals, and non-profit organizations often offer in-person support groups for caregivers.

Online Groups: Online support groups provide the flexibility to connect with others from the comfort of your home. These groups can be found on social media platforms, forums, and specialized websites.

Counseling and Therapy

Individual Counseling: One-on-one counseling with a licensed therapist can help you process your emotions, develop coping strategies, and improve your mental health.

Family Counseling: Family counseling can help address dynamics and conflicts within the family related to caregiving. It can also provide a space for family members to express their feelings and concerns.

Group Therapy: Group therapy offers the benefits of both support groups and professional counseling. It provides a structured environment to discuss your experiences and learn from others.

Joining a support group was a transformative experience for me. It provided a safe space to share my feelings and receive support from others who understood my journey. Counseling also helped me develop coping strategies and maintain my mental health. The combined support from the group and individual therapy made a significant difference in my ability to manage caregiver stress.

Taking care of your emotional and mental health is essential in your role as a caregiver. By recognizing the signs of burnout, implementing stress management techniques, finding joy and maintaining well-being, and seeking support through groups and counseling, you can navigate the challenges of caregiving with resilience and hope. Remember, caring for yourself is not a luxury but a necessity to provide the best care for your loved one. In the next chapter, we will explore practical tips for managing medical care and working with healthcare professionals. Stay strong, and know that you are not alone on this journey.

CHAPTER 7: ACTIVITIES AND ENGAGEMENT

Engaging individuals with dementia in meaningful activities is essential for their cognitive, physical, and emotional well-being. Activities can provide stimulation, enjoyment, and a sense of purpose, helping to maintain their abilities and enhance their quality of life. In this chapter, we will explore cognitive stimulation activities, physical exercise and movement, sensory and creative activities, and how to adapt activities for different stages of dementia. I will also share my personal experiences to provide practical insights and suggestions.

Cognitive Stimulation Activities

Cognitive stimulation activities are designed to engage the brain, improve cognitive function, and provide mental exercise. These activities can help slow cognitive decline and improve mood and behavior.

Types of Cognitive Stimulation Activities

Puzzles and Games: Simple puzzles, crosswords, and memory games can be enjoyable and mentally stimulating. Choose activities that match the individual's cognitive abilities to avoid frustration.

Reading and Storytelling: Reading books, newspapers, or magazines, and engaging in storytelling can help maintain language skills and stimulate memories.

Music and Singing: Listening to music, singing, or playing simple instruments can evoke memories and emotions, providing cognitive and emotional benefits.

Reminiscence Therapy: Discussing past experiences, looking at old photographs, and reminiscing about significant life events can stimulate memory and conversation.

Brain Training Apps: There are various apps designed to provide cognitive stimulation through games and exercises. These can be a fun way to engage the brain.

My mother loved doing crossword puzzles. Even as her dementia progressed, we adapted the puzzles to simpler versions to keep her engaged. We also spent time looking through old photo albums, which sparked conversations and brought back many cherished memories.

Physical Exercise and Movement

Physical exercise is vital for maintaining physical health, mobility, and overall well-being. It can also help reduce symptoms of anxiety and depression, which are common in individuals with dementia.

Types of Physical Exercise

Walking: A simple and effective form of exercise that can be done indoors or outdoors. Walking provides cardiovascular benefits and helps maintain mobility.

Chair Exercises: For those with limited mobility, chair exercises offer a safe way to stay active. These exercises can include seated marching, arm lifts, and leg extensions.

Dancing: Dancing to favorite music can be a joyful and stimulating activity that promotes physical movement and coordination.

Tai Chi and Yoga: Gentle forms of exercise like Tai Chi and yoga can improve balance, flexibility, and relaxation. Many of these exercises can be modified to be done while seated.

Gardening: Light gardening activities such as planting flowers, watering plants, and weeding can provide physical exercise and a sense of accomplishment.

Gardening was one of my mother's favorite activities. Even as her dementia progressed, she enjoyed watering plants and arranging flowers. These activities provided physical exercise and sensory stimulation, as well as a sense of purpose.

Sensory and Creative Activities

Sensory and creative activities engage the senses and stimulate creativity, providing enjoyment and emotional expression. These activities can be particularly beneficial for individuals in the later stages of dementia.

Types of Sensory and Creative Activities

Art and Craft: Painting, drawing, knitting, and other crafts allow for creative expression. The focus should be on the process rather than the end product to ensure the activity is enjoyable.

Sensory Boxes: Create sensory boxes filled with different textured items such as sand, fabric, or beans. These can stimulate the senses and provide a calming effect.

Aromatherapy: Using essential oils like lavender or eucalyptus can provide sensory stimulation and promote relaxation.

Cooking and Baking: Simple cooking and baking activities, such as mixing ingredients or decorating cookies, engage multiple senses and can be very satisfying.

Animal Therapy: Interacting with animals, whether through pet therapy or visiting a petting zoo, can provide sensory stimulation and emotional comfort.

Art projects were a wonderful way for my mother to express herself. Even when her verbal communication became limited, she enjoyed painting and coloring. We also used aromatherapy with lavender oil to help her relax in the evenings, which had a soothing effect.

Adapting Activities for Different Stages

As dementia progresses, the ability to engage in activities may change. Adapting activities to match the individual's abilities and interests is crucial for their continued enjoyment and participation.

Early Stage Dementia

Maintain Routine: Continue with familiar activities but be flexible to accommodate changing abilities.

Introduce New Hobbies: This is a good time to introduce new hobbies that might become sources of joy and stimulation in later stages.

Focus on Social Interaction: Activities that involve social interaction, such as group exercise classes or book clubs, can be particularly beneficial.

Middle Stage Dementia

Simplify Tasks: Simplify activities to match their abilities. For example, use larger puzzle pieces or choose simpler games.

Provide Structure: Structured activities with clear instructions and steps can help reduce confusion and frustration.

Use Visual and Verbal Cues: Provide visual aids and verbal cues to help guide the individual through activities.

Late Stage Dementia

Focus on Sensory Stimulation: Activities that engage the senses, such as listening to music, looking at picture books, or tactile activities, can be very calming and enjoyable.

Encourage Passive Participation: Allow for passive participation in activities, such as watching others garden or listening to a story.

Promote Comfort and Security: Ensure that activities provide a sense of comfort and security. Gentle massage, hand-holding, and other forms of physical touch can be very reassuring.

As my mother's dementia progressed, we had to adapt our activities to her changing abilities. In the early stages, we continued with her favorite hobbies, like gardening and puzzles. In the middle stages, we simplified tasks and provided more guidance. In the later stages, sensory activities like listening to her favorite music and gentle hand massages became important for her comfort and enjoyment.

Engaging individuals with dementia in meaningful activities is crucial for their well-being and quality of life. By focusing on cognitive stimulation activities, physical exercise, sensory and creative activities, and adapting these activities for different stages of dementia, you can help your loved one stay engaged and maintain their abilities. Remember, the goal is to provide enjoyment, stimulation, and a sense of purpose. In the next chapter, we will explore how to manage medical care and work with healthcare professionals effectively. Stay inspired and committed to creating positive experiences for your loved one.

CHAPTER 8: MEDICAL AND HEALTH CARE MANAGEMENT

Managing the medical and health care needs of a loved one with dementia is a critical component of caregiving. Regular health check-ups, managing co-existing medical conditions, working with healthcare professionals, and understanding hospice and palliative care are essential aspects of ensuring your loved one's well-being. This chapter will explore these topics in detail, providing practical advice and insights drawn from my personal experiences.

Regular Health Check-ups

Regular health check-ups are vital for monitoring the overall health and well-being of individuals with dementia. These check-ups help detect and manage potential health issues early, ensuring timely intervention and appropriate care.

Importance of Regular Health Check-ups

Early Detection of Health Issues: Regular visits to the doctor can help identify health problems early, before they become severe.

Medication Management: Regular check-ups provide an opportunity to review and adjust medications, ensuring they are effective and minimizing side effects.

Monitoring Cognitive Function: Health check-ups allow for ongoing assessment of cognitive abilities, helping track the progression of dementia.

Assessing Physical Health: Regular examinations can detect issues like high blood pressure, diabetes, and other conditions that may affect overall health.

Providing Vaccinations: Keeping up with vaccinations, such as flu and pneumonia shots, is important to prevent illnesses.

Components of a Comprehensive Health Check-up

Physical Examination: A thorough physical exam to assess general health and detect any physical issues.

Cognitive Assessment: Tests to evaluate memory, problem-solving skills, and other cognitive functions.

Blood Tests: Laboratory tests to check for issues such as anemia, thyroid problems, and vitamin deficiencies.

Medication Review: A review of all medications to ensure they are necessary and effective.

Mental Health Evaluation: An assessment of mental health to identify issues like depression or anxiety.

Scheduling regular health check-ups for my mother was a priority. These visits provided a chance to address any emerging health concerns and adjust her care plan accordingly. During one visit, a blood test revealed a vitamin B12 deficiency, which was quickly addressed with supplements, improving her overall well-being.

Managing Co-existing Medical Conditions

Individuals with dementia often have other medical conditions that require careful management. Coordinating care for these coexisting conditions is essential to ensure the best possible quality of life.

Common Coexisting Medical Conditions

Diabetes: Controlling blood sugar levels is essential to avoiding consequences. This includes regular monitoring, medication management, and maintaining a healthy diet.

Heart Disease: Regular cardiovascular check-ups, medication adherence, and lifestyle modifications are necessary to manage heart disease.

Arthritis: Pain management, physical therapy, and appropriate medications can help manage arthritis symptoms and maintain mobility.

Hypertension: Monitoring blood pressure, taking prescribed medications, and making dietary changes are key to managing hypertension.

Depression and Anxiety: Mental health conditions require appropriate treatment, which may include therapy and medication.

Strategies for Managing Co-existing Conditions

Coordinated Care: Working closely with all healthcare providers to ensure a coordinated approach to managing multiple conditions.

Medication Management: Keeping a detailed list of all medications and their dosages, and ensuring they are taken as prescribed.

Healthy Lifestyle: Encouraging a healthy diet, regular physical activity, and adequate sleep to support overall health.

Regular Monitoring: Keeping track of symptoms and regularly monitoring health indicators such as blood pressure and blood sugar levels.

Education and Advocacy: Staying informed about the conditions and advocating for the best possible care.

Managing my mother's diabetes alongside her dementia required careful coordination. We worked closely with her primary care physician and a diabetes specialist to monitor her blood sugar levels and adjust her medications as needed. This collaborative approach ensured that both her cognitive and physical health were managed effectively.

Working with Healthcare Professionals

Effective collaboration with healthcare professionals is crucial for managing the health care needs of individuals with dementia. Building strong relationships with doctors, nurses, and other providers ensures comprehensive and coordinated care.

Building a Healthcare Team

Primary Care Physician: A central figure in coordinating care and managing overall health.

Specialists: Depending on the needs, this may include neurologists, cardiologists, endocrinologists, and other specialists.

Nurses and Nurse Practitioners: They often provide direct care and can offer valuable insights into managing health issues.

Social Workers: They can assist with navigating the healthcare system and accessing resources.

Therapists: Physical, occupational, and speech therapists can help maintain mobility, function, and communication skills.

Effective Communication with Healthcare Professionals

Be Prepared: Before appointments, prepare a list of questions and concerns. Bring a list of all medications and any recent health changes.

Take Notes: During appointments, take notes to remember important information and follow-up steps.

Ask Questions: Don't hesitate to ask for clarification if something is unclear. Understanding the care plan is crucial for effective management.

Share Observations: Provide detailed information about any changes in behavior, mood, or physical health.

Follow-Up: Ensure that all recommended follow-up appointments and tests are scheduled and attended.

Building a strong relationship with my mother's healthcare team was essential. Regular communication with her primary care physician and neurologist allowed us to address her evolving needs promptly. During one particularly challenging period, frequent consultations with her doctor helped us manage her increasing agitation by adjusting her medications and implementing new strategies for her care.

Understanding Hospice and Palliative Care

As dementia progresses to advanced stages, understanding hospice and palliative care becomes important. These services focus on comfort, quality of life, and support for both the individual and their family.

What is Palliative Care?

Palliative care refers to specialized medical treatment designed to alleviate the discomfort and anxiety associated with a life-threatening illness. It can be given in conjunction with curative therapies and at any point during the illness.

Symptom Management: Focus on managing symptoms such as pain, agitation, and difficulty breathing.

Emotional Support: Providing emotional and psychological support to the individual and their family.

Improving Quality of Life: Enhancing the overall quality of life by addressing physical, emotional, and spiritual needs.

Coordination of Care: Ensuring that all aspects of care are coordinated and aligned with the individual's preferences.

What is Hospice Care?

Hospice care is a type of palliative care for individuals who are nearing the end of life, typically with a prognosis of six months or less. Rather than curative care, the emphasis is on comfort and quality of life.

Comprehensive Care: Includes medical, emotional, and spiritual support for the individual and their family.

Pain and Symptom Management: Intensive focus on relieving pain and managing symptoms to ensure comfort.

Family Support: Providing support and counseling for family members, including bereavement support.

Home-Based Care: Hospice care is often provided in the individual's home, but it can also be offered in hospice facilities, hospitals, or nursing homes.

Choosing Hospice or Palliative Care

Assessing Needs: Discuss with healthcare providers to assess the individual's needs and determine if palliative or hospice care is appropriate.

Understanding Services: Learn about the services provided by local hospice and palliative care organizations.

Planning Ahead: It's important to have conversations early about the individual's wishes and preferences for end-of-life care.

When my mother's condition reached an advanced stage, we decided to involve hospice care. This decision was not easy, but it provided immense relief and support. The hospice team managed her pain effectively, allowing her to spend her final days in comfort and dignity. They also provided emotional support to our family, guiding us through this difficult time.

Managing the medical and health care needs of a loved one with dementia involves regular health check-ups, addressing co-existing medical conditions, working collaboratively with healthcare professionals, and understanding the options for hospice and palliative care. By staying informed, organized, and proactive, you can ensure that your loved one receives the best possible care. In the next chapter, we will explore the importance of self-care for caregivers and strategies to maintain your own health and well-being. Stay strong and committed to providing compassionate care for your loved one.

CHAPTER 9: ADVANCED CARE PLANNING

As dementia progresses, the needs of your loved one will evolve, requiring thoughtful and compassionate planning for their future care. Advanced care planning involves recognizing the progression of dementia, understanding when to transition to long-term care facilities, making end-of-life plans, and finding bereavement support. This chapter aims to provide you with the knowledge and tools necessary to navigate these critical aspects of caregiving. Through my personal experiences, I hope to offer practical insights and support.

Recognizing the Progression of Dementia

Understanding the stages of dementia and recognizing the signs of progression are crucial for making informed decisions about care.

Early Stage Dementia

Symptoms: Memory lapses, difficulties with complex tasks, and mild changes in behavior and personality.

Care Needs: Support with organization, reminders, and managing daily tasks. promoting independence while offering support when required.

Middle Stage Dementia

Symptoms: Increased memory loss, confusion, difficulty with language, and changes in mood and behavior. The person may need help with daily activities like dressing and eating.

Care Needs: More hands-on care, supervision for safety, and help with personal care. Developing routines and using visual aids can help manage day-to-day life.

Late Stage Dementia

Symptoms: Severe memory loss, inability to recognize loved ones, significant communication difficulties, and physical decline. The person may become bedridden and lose control of bodily functions.

Care Needs: Full-time care, including feeding, bathing, and toileting. Focus on comfort, managing pain, and preventing infections.

As my mother's dementia progressed from the early to the middle stage, it became clear that she needed more help with daily activities. Her increasing confusion and difficulty with simple tasks like making a sandwich or choosing appropriate clothing were signals that we needed to adjust our caregiving approach. Recognizing these changes early allowed us to plan for additional support and resources.

Transitioning to Long-term Care Facilities

Deciding to transition a loved one to a long-term care facility can be one of the most challenging decisions for a caregiver. It's essential to understand when and how to make this transition smoothly.

When to Consider Long-term Care

Increased Care Needs: When the individual's needs exceed what can be safely and effectively provided at home.

Caregiver Burnout: When caregivers are overwhelmed and unable to continue providing care without compromising their health and well-being.

Safety Concerns: When the individual's behavior poses a safety risk to themselves or others, such as frequent wandering or aggression.

Types of Long-term Care Facilities

Assisted Living Facilities: Ideal for people who do not need critical medical attention but need assistance with everyday tasks.

Nursing Homes: Provide 24-hour medical care and assistance with all activities of daily living for those with severe dementia.

Memory Care Units: Specialized facilities within assisted living or nursing homes designed specifically for individuals with dementia, offering tailored care and secure environments.

Selecting the Right Facility

Visit Multiple Facilities: Tour several facilities to compare services, staff-to-resident ratios, cleanliness, and overall atmosphere.

Check Credentials: Ensure the facility is licensed and meets state regulations. Review inspection reports and accreditation status.

Consider Location: Choose a location that is convenient for family and friends to visit regularly.

Evaluate Staff: Observe staff interactions with residents and assess their training and experience in dementia care.

Review Services and Activities: Ensure the facility offers appropriate activities and services that cater to the needs of individuals with dementia.

Transitioning my mother to a memory care unit was a difficult but necessary decision. As her dementia progressed, her care needs became too complex for us to manage at home. Visiting several facilities helped us find a place where she would receive the specialized care she needed. The transition was smoother because we involved her in the process as much as possible, bringing familiar items from home to create a comforting environment.

End-of-Life Planning and Care

End-of-life planning involves making decisions about the type of care and support your loved one will receive as they approach the final stages of dementia. This planning is essential for ensuring their comfort and dignity.

Components of End-of-Life Planning

Advance Directives: Legal documents that outline the individual's preferences for medical treatment, including do-not-resuscitate (DNR) orders and living wills.

Healthcare Proxy: Designating a trusted person to make healthcare decisions on behalf of the individual if they are no longer able to do so.

Palliative care: aims to enhance quality of life and relieve symptoms. It can be provided alongside curative treatment and at any stage of the illness.

Hospice Care: A type of palliative care for individuals nearing the end of life, focusing on comfort rather than curative treatment. Hospice care can be given in a nursing home, a hospice facility, or at the patient's residence.

Discussing End-of-Life Wishes

Open Communication: Have honest and compassionate conversations about end-of-life wishes early in the dementia journey.

Involve the Individual: Whenever possible, involve the person with dementia in these discussions to respect their autonomy and preferences.

Document Decisions: Ensure all decisions are documented in advance directives and shared with healthcare providers and family members.

Having end-of-life discussions with my mother was challenging but necessary. We talked about her wishes early on, which allowed us to make informed decisions when the time came. This planning ensured that her final days were spent in comfort, with her preferences respected.

Bereavement Support

Caring for a loved one with dementia is emotionally taxing, and the grieving process can begin long before their death. Helping caregivers heal and deal with loss is what bereavement support is all about.

Understanding Grief

Anticipatory Grief: The grief experienced before the actual loss, as caregivers witness the gradual decline of their loved one.

Acute Grief: The intense and immediate grief following the death of a loved one.

Complicated Grief: Persistent and severe grief that interferes with daily functioning and requires professional support.

Finding Bereavement Support

Support Groups: Joining a support group for dementia caregivers can provide a sense of community and understanding from others who have experienced similar losses.

Counseling: Professional counseling can help process grief and develop coping strategies.

Family and Friends: Seek out the emotional and practical support of family and friends.

Self-Care: Engage in activities that promote healing, such as exercise, hobbies, and spiritual practices.

After my mother passed away, I found solace in a support group for dementia caregivers. Sharing my experiences with others who understood my journey provided immense comfort. Counseling also helped me navigate the complex emotions of grief and find a path to healing.

Advanced care planning involves recognizing the progression of dementia, making thoughtful decisions about transitioning to long-term care facilities, planning for end-of-life care, and finding bereavement support. By understanding these aspects and preparing accordingly, you can ensure that your loved one receives compassionate and dignified care throughout their journey. In the next chapter, we will discuss the importance of self-care for caregivers and strategies to maintain your own health and well-being. Stay strong and committed to providing the best possible care for your loved one.

CHAPTER 10: RESOURCES AND TOOLS

Navigating the journey of caregiving for a loved one with dementia can be overwhelming, but there are numerous resources and tools available to help you manage this challenging role. This chapter will explore useful books and websites, apps and technology aids, organizations and helplines, and caregiver checklists and worksheets. By leveraging these resources, you can find the support and information needed to provide the best care possible.

Useful Books and Websites

Books and websites can offer invaluable information, guidance, and support for caregivers. They provide a wealth of knowledge on various aspects of dementia care, from understanding the condition to practical caregiving tips.

Books

"The 36-Hour Day" by Nancy L. Mace and Peter V. Rabins

This comprehensive guide is often considered the "bible" for dementia caregivers. It covers a wide range of topics, including the progression of dementia, managing symptoms, and providing daily care.

"Learning to Speak Alzheimer's" by Joanne Koenig Coste

This book offers a practical and empathetic approach to dementia care, emphasizing the importance of communication and understanding the world from the perspective of the person with dementia.

"Creating Moments of Joy Along the Alzheimer's Journey" by Jolene Brackey

This uplifting book provides ideas and strategies for creating positive and joyful moments, even in the face of dementia. It focuses on enhancing the quality of life for both the caregiver and the person with dementia.

Websites

Alzheimer's Association (www.alz.org)

The Alzheimer's Association website offers a vast array of resources, including information on the disease, caregiving tips, support groups, and a 24/7 helpline.

Family Caregiver Alliance (www.caregiver.org)

This website provides resources and support for family caregivers, including fact sheets, webinars, and an online caregiver community.

National Institute on Aging (www.nia.nih.gov)

The NIA website offers research-based information on dementia, caregiving tips, and links to additional resources.

Dementia Care Central
(www.dementiacarecentral.com)

This site provides practical advice on various aspects of dementia care, from understanding the condition to managing daily tasks and accessing financial and legal resources.

Apps and Technology Aids

Technology can play a crucial role in supporting dementia caregivers by providing tools to manage care, stay organized, and connect with others.

Caregiving Apps

CareZone: This app helps caregivers manage medications, keep track of appointments, and store important health information. It also allows you to share updates with family members and other caregivers.

Alzheimers Caregiver Buddy: Created by the Alzheimer's Association, this app provides tips and support for managing common caregiving challenges, along with reminders and resources.

eCare21: This comprehensive caregiving app offers features such as health monitoring, medication management, and care coordination. It can sync with wearable devices to track vital signs and activity levels.

Lotsa Helping Hands: This app allows caregivers to create a community of support by organizing and coordinating help from family and friends. It includes a calendar, message boards, and a place to share updates.

Technology Aids

GPS Trackers: Devices such as GPS watches or tags can help caregivers keep track of loved ones who may wander. These devices can provide real-time location updates and alert you if the person leaves a designated area.

Medication Management Systems: Electronic pill dispensers and reminder systems can help ensure medications are taken correctly and on time. Some systems can send alerts to caregivers if a dose is missed.

Smart Home Devices: Smart home technology, such as voice-activated assistants, can assist with reminders, play calming music, and provide hands-free control of lights and appliances.

Medical Alert Systems: These systems can provide peace of mind by allowing individuals to call for help in an emergency with the push of a button. Some systems also include fall detection and GPS tracking.

Organizations and Helplines

Various organizations and helplines offer support, information, and assistance to dementia caregivers. These resources can provide guidance, connect you with services, and offer emotional support.

Organizations

Alzheimer's Association: The Alzheimer's Association offers support groups, educational programs, and a wealth of online resources. Their local chapters can provide information on services and support available in your area.

Family Caregiver Alliance: This organization provides resources and support for caregivers, including respite care options, educational materials, and an online caregiver community.

AARP Caregiving Resource Center: AARP offers a comprehensive resource center with articles, tools, and support for family caregivers. They also provide information on navigating legal and financial issues related to caregiving.

Eldercare Locator: This public service connects older adults and their families with services and resources in their community. It can help you find local support, from transportation to home care services.

Helplines

Alzheimer's Association 24/7 Helpline (1-800-272-3900): This helpline offers around-the-clock support and information for caregivers. Trained staff can provide guidance on caregiving challenges, resources, and referrals to local services.

National Institute on Aging Information Center (1-800-438-4380): The NIA's helpline offers information on Alzheimer's disease and other dementias, caregiving tips, and research updates.

Caregiver Action Network Caregiver Help Desk (1-855-227-3640): This help desk provides free support for caregivers, offering information and resources to help manage caregiving responsibilities.

Eldercare Locator (1-800-677-1116): This helpline helps connect caregivers with local services and resources, including meal programs, transportation, and in-home care.

Caregiver Checklists and Worksheets

Using checklists and worksheets can help caregivers stay organized, manage tasks, and ensure all aspects of care are covered. These tools can be customized to fit your specific needs and provide a structured approach to caregiving.

Daily Care Checklist

Personal Care: Bathing, dressing, grooming, and toileting.

Medications: Listing all medications, dosages, and times they need to be taken.

Meals and Nutrition: Planning and preparing balanced meals, monitoring food intake.

Activities and Engagement: Scheduling cognitive and physical activities, social interactions.

Health Monitoring: Tracking vital signs, noting any changes in health or behavior.

Emergency Information Worksheet

Personal Information: Name, date of birth, and medical history.

Emergency Contacts: Names, phone numbers, and relationships of primary contacts.

Medical Providers: Contact information for doctors, specialists, and pharmacies.

Medications: A detailed list of all medications, dosages, and prescribing doctors.

Allergies and Conditions: Information on any allergies, chronic conditions, and treatments.

Legal and Financial Planning Checklist

Legal Documents: Ensure all legal documents, such as power of attorney, advance directives, and wills, are in place and up to date.

Financial Accounts: Keep a list of all bank accounts, investment accounts, and insurance policies.

Income and Expenses: Track monthly income and expenses, including medical bills and caregiving costs.

Resources and Benefits: Identify and apply for any benefits or assistance programs available, such as Medicaid or veteran's benefits.

Using checklists and worksheets was a game-changer in managing my mother's care. The daily care checklist ensured that nothing was overlooked, from medications to personal care. The emergency information worksheet provided peace of mind, knowing that all critical information was readily available if needed. Legal and financial planning checklists helped us stay organized and prepared for any eventuality.

Resources and tools are essential for managing the complexities of dementia caregiving. You can improve your caregiving journey and make sure your loved one receives the best care possible by making use of helpful books and websites, utilizing apps and technology aids, connecting with organizations and helplines, and using caregiver checklists and worksheets. In the next chapter, we will delve into strategies for self-care and maintaining your own well-being as a caregiver. Stay committed to providing compassionate care and remember that support and resources are available to help you along the way.

CONCLUSION

As we reach the end of this journey together, I want to take a moment to reflect on the incredible path you've walked as a caregiver for someone with dementia. This book has aimed to be a comprehensive guide, providing you with practical information, resources, and support to navigate the challenges and joys of caregiving. Let's revisit the main points and reaffirm the central message: you are not alone, and with the right tools and mindset, you can provide compassionate and effective care for your loved one.

Caregiving for someone with dementia is an incredibly demanding role, often filled with emotional highs and lows. From understanding the nature of dementia and preparing for the caregiving role to managing daily tasks and advanced care planning, each chapter has provided you with detailed guidance and personal insights.

Recognizing the symptoms and stages of dementia is crucial for planning and providing appropriate care. Knowledge empowers you to anticipate needs and adapt your caregiving approach.

Emotional readiness, building a support network, and addressing legal and financial aspects are foundational steps in your caregiving journey. These preparations help mitigate stress and ensure you are well-equipped to handle the responsibilities.

Managing personal care, medications, nutrition, and creating a routine are essential for maintaining your loved one's quality of life. Practical tips and strategies help make these tasks more manageable and effective.

Effective communication is key to understanding and connecting with your loved one. Learning to handle difficult conversations and understanding non-verbal cues enhances your ability to provide compassionate care.

Understanding and addressing behavioral symptoms, coping with sundowning, and knowing when to seek professional help are critical for maintaining a safe and supportive environment.

Recognizing caregiver burnout, implementing stress management techniques, finding joy, and seeking support are vital for your well-being. Remember, taking care of yourself is just as important as caring for your loved one.

Engaging your loved one in cognitive stimulation, physical exercise, and creative activities enriches their life and supports their overall health. Adapting activities to their abilities and interests fosters positive interactions.

Regular health check-ups, managing co-existing conditions, working with healthcare professionals, and understanding hospice and palliative care ensure comprehensive care for your loved one.

Recognizing the progression of dementia, transitioning to long-term care facilities, and end-of-life planning require thoughtful consideration and preparation. Bereavement support helps you cope with the loss and find healing.

Utilizing books, websites, apps, technology aids, organizations, helplines, and checklists enhances your caregiving capabilities. These resources provide valuable information and support, making your journey more manageable.

The central message of this book is clear: caregiving is a challenging yet profoundly rewarding journey. With the right knowledge, support, and mindset, you can provide the best possible care for your loved one while maintaining your own well-being. Remember, you are not alone. Countless others share your experience, and numerous resources are available to support you.

Your role as a caregiver is invaluable. The love, patience, and dedication you show every day make a significant difference in the life of your loved one. While the journey may be arduous, it is also filled with moments of joy, connection, and fulfillment.

Call to Action

As you close this book, I encourage you to apply the knowledge and strategies you've gained. Here are some steps to take moving forward:

Remain Up to Date: Maintain your education regarding dementia and providing care. Keep abreast of the most recent findings and recommended methodologies.

Build a Support Network: Connect with other caregivers, join support groups, and seek professional guidance when needed. Sharing experiences and receiving support can alleviate the emotional burden.

Prioritize Self-Care: Include self-care as a must in your daily regimen. Participate in enjoyable and soothing activities for yourself. Recall that providing quality care depends on your wellbeing.

Utilize Resources: Take advantage of the resources and tools mentioned in this book. Whether it's using a caregiving app, attending a support group, or reading additional books, these resources can provide valuable assistance.

Plan Ahead: Stay proactive in planning for the future. Address legal and financial aspects, consider long-term care options, and discuss end-of-life wishes with your loved one.

Embrace the Journey: Acknowledge the challenges but also cherish the moments of connection and joy. Celebrate small victories and find meaning in the caregiving experience.

Advocate for Awareness: Spread awareness about dementia and the importance of caregiving. Your experiences can inspire others and contribute to a greater understanding of the condition.

Seek Professional Help When Needed: Don't hesitate to seek professional help for medical, legal, or emotional issues. Professionals can provide expertise and support tailored to your situation.

As you move forward, remember that every step you take is a testament to your strength and dedication. Caregiving is a profound act of love and compassion, and your efforts have a lasting impact.

Writing this book has been a journey of reflection and learning for me as well. Sharing my personal experiences and the knowledge I've gained has been a deeply fulfilling process. I hope that the insights and strategies provided here resonate with you and offer the support you need.

There were moments in my caregiving journey when I felt overwhelmed and uncertain. But through persistence, support, and the right resources, I found a path forward. I want to remind you that it's okay to feel these emotions and to seek help when needed.

Caregiving is a shared journey, and together, we can find strength and resilience.

Final Thoughts

As we conclude this book, I want to leave you with a sense of hope and empowerment. You have embarked on a remarkable journey, one that requires courage, patience, and unwavering love. By equipping yourself with knowledge, seeking support, and caring for your own well-being, you are making a profound difference in the life of your loved one.

Remember, every day is an opportunity to provide care, share love, and create meaningful moments. Embrace this journey with an open heart and a resilient spirit. The road may be challenging, but it is also filled with moments of deep connection and joy.

Thank you for allowing me to be a part of your caregiving journey. I hope this book has provided you with valuable insights and support. As you move forward, may you find strength, peace, and fulfillment in the care you provide.

Stay committed, stay compassionate, and above all, stay hopeful. You are not alone, and by working together, we can gracefully and resiliently navigate the path of providing dementia care.

Finally, caregiving for someone with dementia is a profound and multifaceted journey. By embracing the knowledge, strategies, and resources shared in this book, you can navigate this journey with confidence and compassion. Your dedication and love make a significant difference, and I commend you for your unwavering commitment.

Remember, you are not alone. Reach out for support, prioritize self-care, and continue to educate yourself. Together, we can make the caregiving experience more manageable and fulfilling.

Thank you for being a caregiver. Your efforts are deeply appreciated, and your journey is a testament to the power of love and resilience. As you move forward, may you find joy, peace, and fulfillment in the care you provide.